Harriet Takes the Wheel

Harriet Takes the Wheel

Cathleen O'Connor

Harriet Takes the Wheel
Copyright © 2010 Cathleen O'Connor

Originally published as *Harriet Steps off the Wheel*

StoneSpring, Inc. (2005)

All rights reserved. No part of this book may be reproduced (except for inclusion of excerpts in critical articles or reviews), disseminated or utilized in any form or by any means, electronic or mechanical, including photocopying, recording, or in any information storage and retrieval system, or the Internet/World Wide Web without written permission from the author and publisher. Unauthorized reproduction of any part of this work is illegal and is punishable by law.

Cover and Interior Illustrations by Jo Jayson; www.jojayson.com

ISBN 978-0-557-46872-0

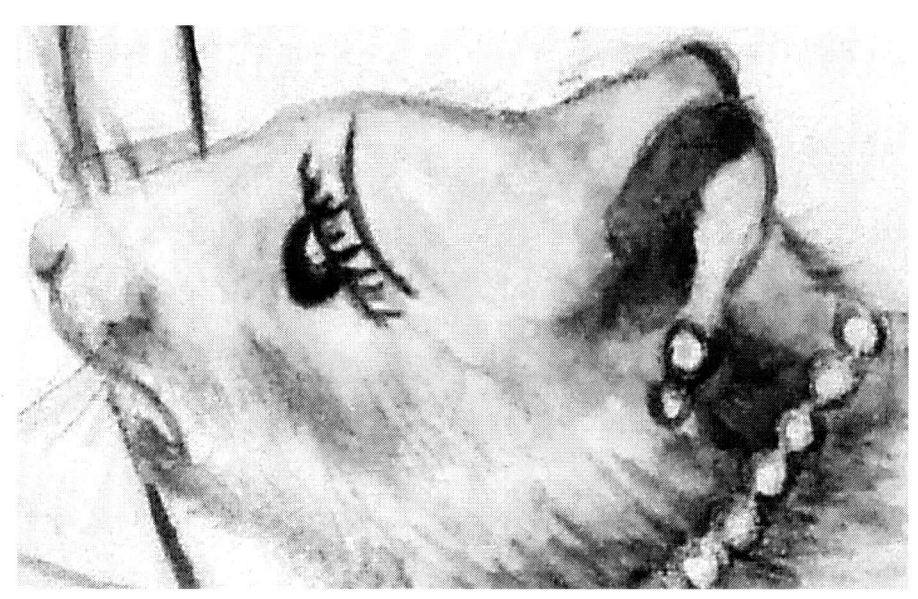

The average hamster weighs just over half a pound.
The average woman is always trying to lose those last twenty hamsters.

Acknowledgements

Inspiration comes from many surprising places – childhood stories, beloved pets, wonderful friends and challenging experiences. Most of all inspiration comes from all the amazing people willing to share their stories and their lives. I am thankful for every woman who became part of Harriet's character and quest for balance. Together we shared laughs and tears; successes and failures; hugs and love. So, to Deb, Ro, Demitra, Lora, Barbara, Helene, Maureen, Eve, Joanne, Carol, Katie and Maryellen – thank you! May you continue to offer your wisdom and love – the world so needs your gifts.

Table of Contents

Introduction:	Welcome from the Author	xi
Chapter 1:	The Book Club Convenes	1
Chapter 2:	The Ever-Present Wheel	7
Chapter 3:	Asking for Help	13
Chapter 4:	Segments of Stress	17
Chapter 5:	Spinning out of Control	23
Chapter 6:	To Do or Not To Do	29
Chapter 7:	Addicted to the Wheel	33
Chapter 8:	The Mysterious Stranger	37
Chapter 9:	As the Wheel Turns	45
Chapter 10:	Taking the Wheel at Home	51
Chapter 11:	Taking the Wheel at Work	57
Chapter 12:	A New Vision	63
Chapter 13:	The Book Club Acts	67
Postscript:	From the Human Behind the Hamster	73

Introduction

Welcome dear reader to a world of small creatures with big problems! Harriet's journey from concept to the current incarnation you read today has been an interesting one. Since Harriet is my alter ego, you may not be surprised to learn that Harriet's transitions and insights have mirrored my own. When I first started out in business (more years ago than I care to remember), I was an eager-to-please go-getter, thirsty for knowledge and experience, and truly excited about my work and the amazing contribution I pictured myself giving to the world. And, of course, I was going to make tons of money at my career, marry the perfectly understanding man and have a lovely home and family. Sound familiar?

More than twenty years later I found myself a successful corporate vice president ensconced in a beautiful corner office overlooking 42nd street in one of the busiest and most exciting cities in the world. I had been privileged to travel the globe and live a lifestyle that was the envy of my friends. My expectations for success had been surpassed again and again. Yet inside something was missing. The funny thing about achieving your dreams is that one day you may wake up and realize those dreams might not have been yours after all. In the midst of my wonderful success, I was working, on average, twelve to fourteen hour days, and found myself burdened with a host of stress-related illnesses. My life was extremely busy and disturbingly empty at the same time.

Little did I know a new dream for my life was taking shape. So, on a late spring morning in 1997 I made the decision that was to start me on a new phase of my journey. I decided to walk away from my successful career and into a void so large that it was frightening to contemplate. Even having made the decision, it took me another year to actually leave and, when I did have that final "goodbye" party, I felt the apprehension of someone stepping off a cliff hoping against hope that there was a ledge just out of sight.

That part of my journey gave birth to Harriet's first foray into the public domain with the publishing of *Harriet Steps Off the Wheel* in 2005. In the time since I left my corporate career, I opened a holistic wellness center, pursued my interest in spirituality by becoming an ordained metaphysical minister and followed a new dream of entrepreneurship. A lot of life lessons came my way through owning my own business, especially around boundaries that were unhealed in my life having to do with over-giving of my time and my financial resources. These issues were with me in my corporate job but, in that job, I was rewarded for the very patterns that were causing me difficulty as an entrepreneur. Ultimately the business did not succeed as I hoped it would and once I realized I would not continue in it I was lost looking for what I was meant to do in the world.

During that time I was playing around with changes to the Harriet story and had re-titled my little fable, *Harriet Re-Invents the Wheel*. Again, Harriet was mirroring my own process of self-discovery and re-invention. But re-invention was not the avenue I eventually would pursue. I started taking classes – art classes, singing lessons, writing retreats and even graphic design. And I finally remembered the original dream – the original purpose of my life – as a creative person in the world. And that is where you find Harriet and I today – firmly in charge of the co-creative process of life.

So now you will be reading that *Harriet Takes the Wheel* and so she does, as have I. Think of Harriet as a guide on your journey. Harriet reminds all of us that, to create the life we want, we have to consciously honor and respect ourselves each and every day, by making room for our relationships, our wonderful work, our health, our creative play, and our spirit—all the elements that make up the very core of who we are. Harriet was only able to take charge of the wheel she was on (i.e., her world) when she fully understood that the changes she was about to make were not about *restricting* life but rather about opening it up to what really matters. And once we know what really matters, we have the ability and willingness (and yes, sometimes even the courage) to say "NO"—and mean it.

I like to think that Harriet's little story is in essence a parable about personal freedom; about shaking off the shackles of other people's expectations and finding the spectacular event of a single life, lived with conscious choice.

Enjoy the journey!

Chapter 1

The monthly book club had just started when Rosemary rushed in late from work, still talking into her headset while simultaneously thumbing through her texts.

"I'm sorry!" she announced to no one in particular, her voice changing timber as she looked at her Blackberry™, "Listen to this tweet from the DailyCalm", she said with a note of incredulity. "The people that annoy you the most at work are blessed mirrors of your own magnificence."

"Seriously!!??!!"

"I mean – seriously??!!"

The rest of the book club members had started laughing as Rosemary's eyes widened and her lips formed a half-smile, half-smirk.

"I suppose that means that Larry who didn't get the sales figures to me on time, for the *millionth* time, today is just mirroring my desire to magnificently throw him out the office window! And, believe me, I could do it magnificently!"

By now, Lori was almost rolling off the couch with laughter, tears forming at the corners of her eyes. As she gathered herself together, she managed to gasp out, "Ro, why do you subscribe to that website, anyway? It doesn't seem to be having the calming effect I'm assuming it's supposed to inspire."

Lori wiped the tear drops from the corners of her eyes, her face still wearing a broad smile.

"I subscribed because I'm trying to bring some calm and balance into my crazy, hectic life." Rosemary smiled back, fully realizing how funny her arrival and reaction to the tweet had been. "If I couldn't come here once a month and laugh about my life, I'd sink into the abyss like everyone else in my office."

"Which abyss is that?" Jane asked. "Personally, I like to wallow in the abyss of procrastination and stagnation periodically, just to catch up on my sleep. I find after a few good days of real inertia I can move on to the abyss of perpetual overwhelm."

"Wasn't that one of the novenas from school?" Mary asked. "I'm sure I remember praying to Our Lady of Perpetual Overwhelm. If not, I'm going to start today!"

Still laughing, Laura, who was hosting this month's book club, tried to get the group back on track. Looking around she said, "you know – this is the first time in a long while that we are all together for our meeting. I don't suppose anyone has actually read the book?" Several sheepish faces looked back at her, answering what had become an almost rhetorical question over the last few months.

"What was the book, anyway?" Jill asked, setting off another round of laughter.

"Believe it or not," Laura said, "we chose *Great Expectations*. I think we were thinking that reading some classics would get us going again."

"Oh, goody – Dickens!" Rosemary said. "Now there's some light reading to help us climb out of the abyss! Unrealistic expectations are more like it. That must have been what we were feeling when we made that selection! I have enough expectations to deal with in my life, great and otherwise. I don't need any more!"

Rosemary's words were met with murmurs of agreement from all the women present.

"I agree," Jane said, "there just aren't enough hours in the day to meet all the demands on my time. And it seems as soon as we start off in one direction at work, someone on top changes his mind and off we go in another direction. We never seem to get a period where things just settle down."

"I know just what you mean." Ronnie shared. "It's like someone set the treadmill on high, somehow tricked us into getting on, and now we can't find the off switch."

Everyone laughed at Ronnie's analogy and story after story began to pour out. Most of the women present were successful, well-paid corporate executives, business owners, managers or professionals – just the group you'd expect to be energized and enthusiastic about what they had achieved. Lily even ran her own company, one that had been growing very successfully. Even with that, the feelings expressed by the majority present were just the opposite of what one would have thought. Fatigue, anxiety and stress seemed to sap the joy from jobs and lives that had once held excitement and purpose. It wasn't any one thing, per se, but a mix of factors surrounding their experience of work and home – factors over which they felt little control.

Just last year, because of what she saw as the unrelenting pressure to maintain a career and take care of her growing family, Laura had left her high-level job with a global consulting firm. Since that time Laura seemed like a new person – more relaxed, happier and, most of all, energized. So it came as a surprise to everyone when Laura spoke up.

"You know I used to think that all my problems were caused by the company and a never-ending workload. And it's true in the current climate that corporate boards seem to give top management greater and greater compensation and options while the rest of the company is being told to tighten their belts and make do with less. I know my company spent millions rolling out new corporate values programs yet business seemed to go on just as before. Truth was I felt disenchanted and not really valued and appreciated for all the hard work I put in.

Being home this past year has allowed me a sense of perspective I didn't have when I was in the trenches, burning out from overwork. I've come to see the problem differently and think if given the opportunity now I would approach my job and my life in a new way. It's easy to focus on the negative and certainly with all the sweeping reengineering, layoffs and mergers happening in business, there have been significant changes, not all of them positive. But I see things from a more balanced view now. Certainly the company has responsibilities for the pace and amount of work required, but the individual also has responsibilities to define good boundaries around those same elements."

"Oh, come on Laura," Jane was saying, "It's easy for you to have a different perspective *now* when you aren't in the day-to-day of it. And I know you'll agree you were fortunate to have the option to choose to stay home and be a full-time mother. Not everyone can, and I don't see how we, as individuals, have any real control over the situation. It's well-known, though no one says it outright, that to get ahead today or just make ends meet, you have to be willing to make work the main priority. Companies talk about work/life balance, but I see it as just another 'flavor-of-the-month' program pushed by human resources. The real expectations haven't changed and you are penalized if you are seen to not always be available and ready to do whatever is asked. Let's face it. We work for workaholics who expect everyone else to be the same."

The group nodded their heads and Ronnie spoke up again. "I agree with Jane. I feel constantly torn because of the time I have to spend at my job and not at home with my son. I don't feel I have a choice. Both my husband and I have to work – it isn't an option – and that means lots of time away from home and away from our son. I don't get through a single day without feeling guilty every time I think about him, and I worry what he will think when he's older about parents who weren't able to be there for him the way my mother was for me when I was growing up."

"Look at us!" Jane said more earnestly. "Several of us here are the directors and senior management of the organizations we work for. If we feel this way, when we are supposed to have more control over what happens, imagine how everyone who works for us must feel. I have tried repeatedly to honor the work/life needs of my staff but find they are just as caught up in the problem as I am, especially the women. And I truly don't know how I can help to make it better. When you talk about the company's responsibility, Laura, you are talking about us. We're just as responsible for our failure to find good work/life options for our staff as we are unable to find them for ourselves."

Laura nodded, seeing she had really touched a sore point with the group.

"How about we deviate from our planned program and try a book I just came across as our read for tonight? It's a small book called *Harriet Takes the Wheel*, and it's a little parable about work and life balance. Reading it is what got me thinking about what choices I had and still have in creating a life that works for me. What do you say I read it to the group, and we use our remaining time to brainstorm together how we can support each other in making some changes to address the problem? It can't hurt, can it? Certainly it's better than the familiar griping session we manage to have every month. And while griping is satisfying on a certain level, it doesn't really allow us the opportunity to move things in a more positive direction."

"I'm willing," Ronnie said as Rosemary, Lily and the other members nodded their heads in agreement. Jane was the most skeptical.

"I'm willing to try," she said, "but don't really expect any big light bulbs will go on for me. And more and more I am seeing that this is not just a problem for us women. I think for many of the younger men whose fathers were absent pursuing careers when they were growing up, not being there for their own children is just not acceptable."

"I agree with you fully, Jane." Laura said. "Even though this book is told from the female perspective, there is a larger picture in mind of the effects on families as a whole. I'm sure we can all learn from our heroine's experience. By the way, did I mention that Harriet is a hamster?"

Smiling at the raised eyebrows of the group, Laura began to read.

Chapter 2

Deep in the burrow, Harriet snuggled down under the fragrant shavings of her bed, trying to cling to images of strawberries that were in her mind as she woke. For some reason she had been craving strawberries lately – her favorite treat. Sighing, she stretched her arms and flexed her buff-colored paws, reaching for an elusive moment of peace and quiet before starting her day. Instead, her morning silence fractured as screeching sounds made by Mitzi and Bud, her incredibly vocal hamster pups, reached her ears. Then she heard the low rumble of her mate Walter's angry growl as he tried to bring the pups under control and get them ready to go off to school.

Harriet never just woke up anymore rested and restored from a good night's sleep. Why, she couldn't even remember the last time she had slept through the night and awoke refreshed and ready to face a new day. As Mitzi's voice reached a new pitch, Harriet dragged herself out of bed, fluffed her fur and stood looking into her wardrobe, hoping the cacophony in the kitchen would subside if she delayed long enough. As she continued to get ready for her day, she wondered how her life had gotten to this point. She seemed to have no energy for anything anymore – not for her family, not for her job, not for dinners with friends and, certainly, not for herself.

As Harriet combed through her fur looking for any telltale signs of gray, she heard her pager beep – probably that email from overseas that had been promised the day before. Harriet glanced at her ever-present pager and, for a moment – just one brief exhilarating moment – she pictured herself smashing it into the teeniest, tiniest bits imaginable. She returned to reality just as the noise finally leveled off downstairs and she heard the scampering of little hamster feet running through the tunnels, again late for school. If she didn't hurry up, she herself was going to miss the 7 o'clock burrow express and her 8 o'clock meeting with the market research team for Seeds International.

*****

From the train, as it pulled into the station, Harriet could see the big wheel outside Seeds International, resplendent in its size and gold tones; the 'wheel of progress' as it was called. Under the Seeds International sign was the company's new slogan: *Sow Your Seeds with Us*. The big wheel and the park-like property around it was the site of many celebrations that the company held throughout the year. Harriet was thinking about the last Hamster Health Screening Day and the chaos that ensued when Hermione, a hamster with a particularly low threshold for needles and pinpricks, had fainted while waiting on line to give blood. Harriet hadn't given blood that day – something about seeing poor Hermione sprawled out in front of the big wheel in such an undignified manner had stopped her cold.

"I feel like I've given enough blood!" she had said to no one in particular and had gotten off the line and returned to her desk.

Harriet was drawn out of her reverie by the commotion caused by the sounds of hundreds of hamsters exiting the train. On the way into the building, Harriet stopped to get her favorite sunflower seed mix from the vending machine in the lobby. Harriet had long ago given up breakfast as a meal unto itself. She basically lived on the snacks and drinks she got from the vending machines, the food carts and the quick trips to the company cafeteria during lunchtime. She had gained an extra few ounces over the past few years and was noticeably more sluggish as she got older but just attributed that to the normal effects of age. She didn't know any hamsters that were as energetic at her age as when they were young and starting fresh in the world.

Willy, Sten and Parci were all in the conference room when Harriet walked in for the meeting. Parci was writing the agenda on the white board, while Sten was attempting to get the video working in order to conference in their hamster colleagues at the European Headquarters.

Harriet looked around the room at the frenetic efforts of Sten and Parci and asked Willy, "is it just me, or are we spending more and more time rushing around, accomplishing less and less?"

"It's not just you, Harriet." Willy replied, "The important thing is that we are seen to be rushing around. That's what impresses management."

Harriet shook her head and took her place at the table. Just then video came in of Bruno, her Siberian hamster counterpart. He was sitting so close to the webcam that all Harriet could see was two big popping eyes surrounded by silky black fur.

"Bruno! Bruno!" Harriet tried to get his attention. "You look like a gerbil on wildflower weed. You're too close to the webcam. Back up or we'll have nightmares for weeks!"

Ignoring the insult, Bruno snorted and slid his stool back until he was once again just a normal hamster on the video and the other members of his team came into view. Two hours later, the fur was literally flying as Harriet and Bruno continued to debate the company's approach to their new marketing slogan. The new slogan, *Sow Your Seeds with Us*, was supposed to make the customer feel part of the company and incite them to invest in Seeds International as a good business opportunity. Harriet wasn't a fan of the new slogan but it was her group's job to get the other divisions on board.

Harriet looked over at Sten and Parci who were busily gnawing on a stack of pencils. Keeping pencils in stock was a continual challenge at Seeds International as whenever nerves frayed, gnawing ensued. As she listened to her counterpart go on about the European interpretation of *seeds*, Harriet thought to herself: "So now not only do we want our customers to eat our product and pay for the privilege, we also want them to finance it as well!"

She caught herself in the midst of her cynical thought, realizing that when she was younger she hadn't had such an edge. She used to have enthusiasm and interest in her work and vitality at home. What had happened, she wondered. What truly had happened?

"Harriet . . . Harriet . . . **Harriet!**" Sten broke her reverie, having whittled the last pencil down to the eraser. "Do you agree we should table our discussions for now and allow the European team to research the cultural meaning of *seeds* further before going forward?"

"Oh, great!" Harriet thought, "Another massive waste of time and resources."

But, all she said was, "Agreed. Bruno, we'll hear back from you in two weeks."

With that the group agreed; the meeting was completed; and, once again, no progress was made. Harriet took her burgeoning headache back to her office and closed the door. She was noticing that she was increasingly cranky and impatient with the normally tedious pace of progress, and she was beginning to wonder if perhaps she needed some time off. Harriet decided on the spot to see her hamster resources representative that very afternoon. She needed to talk to someone, and the staff in the Hamsters Capital Management Group was there for precisely that purpose.

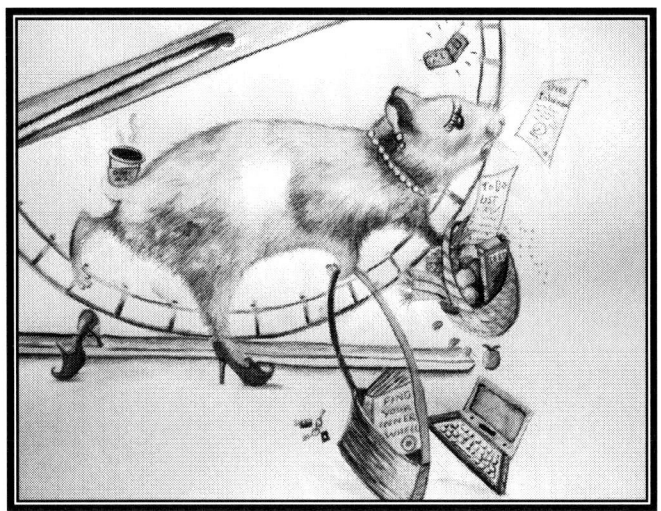

Take the Wheel

Exercise Your Power of Intention

Start each day with a conscious choice to set intentions about how you want your day to go. Think about one thing that if you got it done that day would leave you feeling good about yourself. Make one intention for your day and make it something that nurtures you as well as others. Your *Power of Intention* gets those creative juices flowing and sets the tone for whatever happens that day.

Chapter 3

After lunch, Harriet arrived on time at the office of Percy, her hamster resource representative, for her consultation. Percy wasn't in but was expected back soon Harriet was told by his energetic assistant, Molly. Twenty minutes later Percy showed up, nodding to Harriet to come in while offering a facile apology for his tardiness. All apologies from Percy had something to do with hamsters more important than whoever was waiting for him, and that of course, included Harriet.

"Well," said Percy once Harriet was seated, "it's so good to see you, Harriet. What can I do for you?"

"Well, I'm not sure exactly where to begin," Harriet began.

"Begin wherever you want, Harriet," Percy interrupted, "I've always found it best to lay my cards straight up on the table. We're a team here, Harriet – one for all and all for one. We only get to the end zone by passing the ball and supporting each other."

Harriet was already thinking that if Percy uttered many more patently untrue platitudes like that to her, she would have to do something drastic. Harriet felt Percy's eyes upon her and realized he was waiting for her to continue.

"As I was saying," Harriet began again, "lately I've felt as if I can't do anything right. I feel overwhelmed by the demands at the office, the continual need for overtime, the pups' schedules and needs, trying to keep a good home and still manage some time for my husband, Walter."

Percy looked decidedly uncomfortable.

"Harriet," Percy said, holding up one hand, "I think I have to stop you here. You are bringing a lot of personal matters into the discussion. Now, you know very well that work is work and your personal life is your personal life. If there is a work problem you have, I'd be happy to help you, but as to the personal matters, I can only refer you to the HAP (Hamsters Assistance Program) which is staffed with specialists qualified to help you sort out your personal life."

"I'm not trying to sort out my personal life, Percy," Harriet said, exasperated, "I'm trying to figure out how one manages to get it all done and keep everyone satisfied in the process."

"Ah," said Percy, "now I can help you. The secret, Harriet, is time management. You just need proper time management so you can allocate the time you need during the day to your various activities."

Harriet was skeptical but she was feeling so bad about herself she was willing to try anything. Percy was up from behind his desk, sorting through his files, and returned with a form for a time management seminar being offered at the company later that week.

"Here's your solution, Harriet," Percy said proudly, ushering Harriet to the door as he spoke, "I'll sign you up and you'll be organized and on your way in no time at all."

Harriet stood outside Percy's closed door with the time management seminar form in hand. Something deep inside her doubted that this was the answer but she didn't know what the answer was. Harriet decided she would try the seminar. After all, perhaps it would help. Even if it helped just a little, Harriet figured, that had to be better than what she was doing on her own.

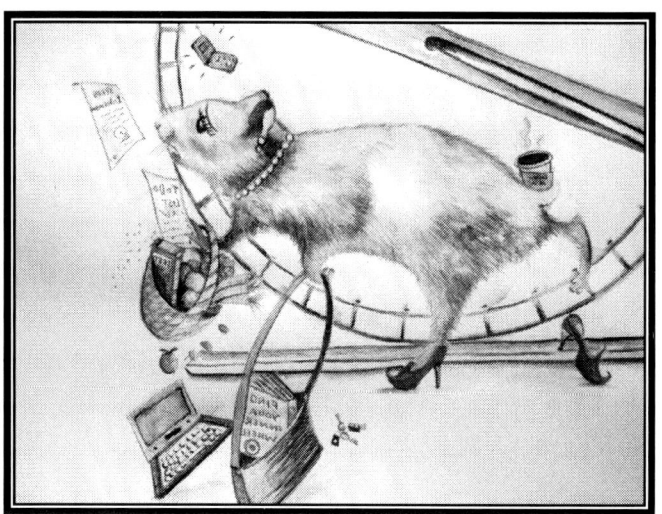

Take the Wheel

Trust the Power of Your Intuition

Inside of you is a deep knowingness about what you need to feel fulfilled and happy in your life. You can connect with that wise part of yourself through your *Power of Intuition*. Your intuition is that little voice or sense that lets you know the "truth" in any situation, even the truth of your own heart. Only you can truly know what is in your deepest best interest.

Chapter 4

Harriet wriggled into a chair in the back of the room just as the time management specialist, Jubee, was extolling the virtues of what she called the segmented work day. She was enthusiastic in her presentation. As she stood at the front of the room, her round eyes sparkled and her golden fur shone under the meeting room lights.

"Well, she's *definitely* not stressed!" Harriet thought to herself as Jubee continued.

"No one," Jubee was saying, "can be organized and manage their time without a proper segmentation approach. For example, let's say you have to prepare a proposal for a new product marketing plan. You know the due date and you know what you have to do. Let's work with this example to see how we segment the day to get things done without stress or confusion."

She turned to Harriet, who had a bit of a glazed look in her eyes.

"Harriet," she began, "list some of the tasks that would need to be done to prepare the marketing plan proposal."

Harriet quickly rattled off, "you'd need a product concept, market research analyses, focus group panels, media analyses as to which media would be most effective, creative development and production estimates, a product launch timeline, post-launch customer feedback . . ."

Jubee raised a paw to silence Harriet at that point.

"Ok, Harriet, let's take one aspect – let's choose media analyses and assume you needed to get that done. On your calendar you would slot in 15 minutes per day for media analyses for as many days as you need. That is what we mean by segmentation. You just allow the time in your day and make sure you adhere to it and . . . **_Like Magic!_** . . . you are done and not feeling at all stressed."

Harriet looked at Jubee as if she were crazy.

"But," Harriet was saying, "no one can do a media analysis in 15 minutes. It's completely unreasonable!"

"Harriet, Harriet," Jubee patiently said, "segmentation is predicated on the principle that we waste most of our day doing things we don't need to do. So, if you really allot the time and focus, focus, focus, it works, believe me."

"Waste the day?!" Harriet said, feeling herself getting angry, "I don't waste any of my days but a lot of it is wasted for me! You can't do a proper media analysis in 15 minutes no matter how much you focus!"

"Harriet," Jubee said calmly, "I think you're missing the point. You don't have to do the entire media analysis in one day. You just allocate your 15 minutes, stop where you are and continue in your next 15-minute block the following day."

"But what about meetings, other people you need to involve, the time it takes just to create the spreadsheets for the analyses . . . ," Harriet was rattling off the steps as fast as she could.

"Just try it, Harriet," Jubee said, "it will only make sense once you segment your entire day. Try it for a week and then come back and tell me you are happier, more organized and productive than you've ever been. Remember, class, '*Segment Your Stress.*' Let's say the slogan together.

"Segment Your Stress!" the class enthusiastically shouted.

* * * * *

It was 6am and Harriet was looking at her segmented work schedule for the day. There, carefully broken down into 15 minute time-periods, were the activities the specialist suggested after reviewing Harriet's responsibilities and deadlines:

> ## **Harriet Hamster's Stress-Free Schedule!**
>
> 9:00am – Welcome to Your Productive New Day!
> 9:15am – Answer Overnight Emails
> 9:30am – Answer Overnight Overseas Phone Messages
> 9:45am – File papers from yesterday's meetings
> 10:00am – Take items in the inbox, read and allocate either to *Do Now, Do Later, File, Throw Out, Send On*
> 10:30am - Attend market research team meeting
> 11:30am – Analyze tasks and schedule time the next day for the first item in the *Do Later* file.
> 11:45am – Analyze tasks and schedule time the next day for the second item in the *Do Later* file.
> 12:00 – 1:00pm – Healthy Lunch
> 1:00pm – Write notes on the *Send On* items and send them on. Take new items in Inbox and allocate them by category
> 1:15 – 2:30pm – Continue on with same process as in the morning. Get those phone messages and emails returned!
> 2:30pm – Afternoon break for snack and beverage
> 2:45pm – 4:30pm – Major project work
> *'We like to end the day on a note of accomplishment!'*
> 4:30pm – Clean off desk, organize papers and leave a fresh, clean space for the morning. Whatever is unfinished is left.
> 5:00pm – Leave the office for a stress-free night at home. *Enjoy!*

Just looking at the schedule got Harriet's stomach tied up in knots. It was a dizzying list of minor and major activities compressed into what seemed to be completely illogical groupings. However, she had agreed to try the new approach so she started right in with those overseas emails, having already stuffed her pouches with as many sunflower seeds as she could. After all, Harriet reasoned, there was the remote chance this just might just work. It certainly held the promise that she would be home on time for once and able to spend time with Walter and the pups.

By 10:00am Harriet was in deep distress. She was still on a phone call to London that she started at 9:30am, the first overseas overnight phone call she was returning in her segmented block of time. She hurriedly got off the phone and rushed, late of course, into the market research meeting which ran late and right through her segmented lunch break. It was now 2:00pm. Harriet just had time to wolf down a few seed packets from the vending machine and she was back at her desk trying desperately to find the first *Do Now* item in the Inbox, when her boss called to get the latest figures on the product marketing campaign for the new mixed seeds line. Scurrying around the office, Harriet got the information to him just as her secretary, Minnie, stuck her head in the door to report that Mitzi's school was on the line with an emergency. It seems Mitzi was not feeling well and either she or Walter had to come pick her up. At 3:00pm on the first of her segmented work days, Harriet, a furball of stress, found herself rushing for the train to get to Mitzi's school. Oh well, there was always tomorrow.

The next day of segmentation didn't fare any better than the first, except that now Harriet was behind with two days worth of emails to answer, phone calls to be returned, files to be made and meetings to attend. Somewhere around the fourth day of her segmented work week Harriet realized that she had not done any actual *work* in the previous three days. Oh sure, she had answered a few phone calls, a few emails, pushed paper from the Inbox into a few stacks of paper but no actual work had taken place. Harriet's segmented work day held no time for actual work to be done.

"Interesting," Harriet thought to herself, "if I keep with this plan, I should be completely unproductive in just another few days."

The one thing the approach had done was what it had promised. Her stress was now segmented. Instead of getting stressed at certain times over certain things during the day, Harriet was now stressed in 15-

minute chunks. After a few days with her schedule Harriet looked like a furry ball that had been stuck in a light socket. In a flash of inspiration she deliberately and ceremoniously chewed her schedule to bits. She could always use the shavings to patch holes in the burrow tunnels.

"Ah, recycled stress," Harriet mused. At least something productive had come from her efforts.

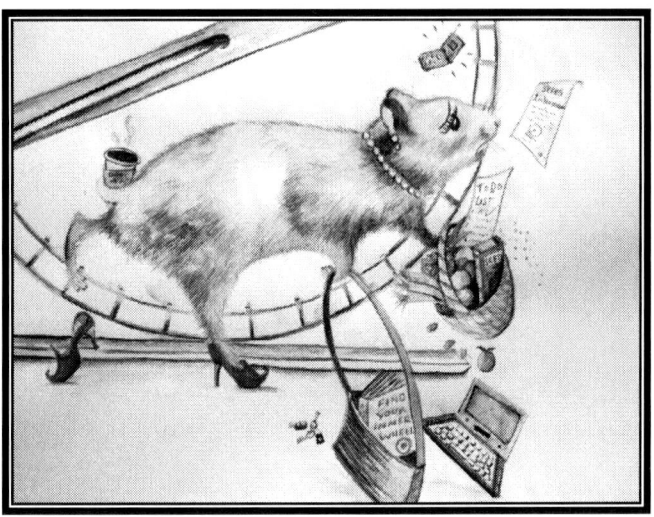

Take the Wheel

Embrace Priority Power!

Think about what the priorities are in your life. Are you even on your own list? When you embrace your *Priority Power*, you exercise the healthy boundaries of someone who knows her limits. At work, priorities are vital to staving off overwhelm; and they are just as vital in your personal life. Use your priority power to see where you are spending your energy and time and adjust accordingly. Think energy, not time, management!

Chapter 5

Okay, so time management was not the answer Harriet was seeking, but what was? After giving up the segmentation approach and returning to her former methods, Harriet was a little disillusioned that she would ever find the answer to her problem. At lunch she mentioned how she was feeling to her friend, Bootsie, who always seemed to have lots of excess energy and vitality.

"Harriet, darling," said Bootsie sympathetically, "I wish you had come to me right away. The answer is so simple. You just have to incorporate exercise into your workday as a way to eliminate the stresses that build up. Exercise makes you feel so invigorated and good about yourself, that the day just flies by. Why don't you join me in the lunchtime spinning class down in the fitness center? You'll see what I mean."

Harriet considered what Bootsie said. Certainly Bootsie, the most energetic bundle of fur Harriet had ever seen, seemed to have vitality to spare. Harriet also noticed that Bootsie rarely stayed late, took extra time at lunch and always seemed to have time in her day to volunteer to help with company outings and special event days.

"Exercise?" thought Harriet. "Could that be what I've needed all along? And at lunchtime, no less? I have put on a few ounces over the years. Perhaps skipping lunch and joining the spinning class will make me feel better."

"Well?" Bootsie was saying, "are you going to join me or not?"

"I will, Bootsie," Harriet said. "I'll meet you at the fitness center tomorrow."

"You won't regret it, Harriet," Bootsie said, "Just you wait. Soon you'll be feeling like your old self."

* * * * *

The next morning Harriet managed to remember to pack her gym clothes to bring to the office. After a particularly busy morning, she met Bootsie in the fitness center just as the spinning class was getting started.

"Find your wheel, everyone," the instructor, Tippin, was saying. "Remember – the wheel is your friend. Become one with the wheel."

Harriet got inside her wheel and started gingerly walking forward to get the hang of the rhythm again. She hadn't really spent time on the wheel since she was a pup but remembered spinning happily when she couldn't sleep. Surely, she would soon regain her ease on the wheel. Just as she was starting to feel comfortable, all four paws moving effortlessly at a steady pace, the instructor blew his whistle to start the class.

"And now – forward spins, 1, 2, 3, 4 . . . and . . . reverse spins, 1, 2, 3, 4 . . . and . . . forward again, 1, 2, 3, 4 . . . and . . . reverse, 1, 2, 3, 4 . . . now forward with hands free, 1, 2, 3, 4 . . . and . . . reverse hands free, 1, 2, 3, 4 . . . and . . ."

Harriet had stopped listening. She was stuck on reverse 1, 2, 3, 4 and hands free was simply not going to happen unless the class was looking forward to a slightly pudgy hamster splattered across the fitness center.

"Why can't I go backwards?" Harriet asked herself, trying again to move on the wheel in reverse. She looked around her and saw Bootsie, her little pink ears bobbing up and down, happily going forwards, reverse, forwards again, hands free – all with the greatest agility and ease. Every time Harriet tried to go backwards, the wheel simply came to a halt with Harriet spread eagled across the rungs.

"This is humiliating," Harriet thought, "when did spinning become this difficult?"

Actually, now that she thought about it, Harriet wondered when spinning had become so complicated that it required an instructor.

Spinning came naturally to hamsters. Every hamster was born to the wheel. It was what made them such good and loyal employees later in life. As the instructor continued to shout directions for forward and reverse, Harriet started to feel a little dizzy. She was feeling as out of control in spinning class as she did with everything else she was trying to do in life. And things were about to get worse.

Tippin had noticed that Harriet was having difficulty and had come over to stand next to her, continuing to shout directions to the class, while grabbing Harriet's arms and legs and moving the wheel backwards. The delicate balance that Harriet had managed on the rungs gave way, and she toppled out of the wheel and landed on top of the instructor with a splat that caught the attention of the other hamsters working out in the fitness center. Next thing she knew, Bootsie and a couple of the others were picking her and Tippin up off the floor and asking if she were all right.

Harriet stared into a sea of concerned and disapproving faces and managed to say:

"Oops! I seem to have spun out of control."

Harriet was pretty pleased with her pun and proud of herself for putting a humorous 'spin' on an embarrassing situation, but it seemed that the devoted spinners weren't especially given to levity during their exercise periods. After the others had gone back to their wheels, Bootsie helped Harriet to a chair in the lounge outside the exercise room.

"Harriet, darling," Bootsie began, "don't get discouraged. Why I was just terrible in the beginning – couldn't do the reverse thing at all, but I stuck with it, practicing sometimes 3-4 hours a day and now look at me!"

"Three to four hours a day," Harriet thought incredulously, "how can she possibly have the time to spend three to four hours a day in the fitness center?"

Bootsie was going on about endorphins and serotonin levels, and Harriet suddenly had the feeling she had landed on an alien world. She just didn't have the same impulse to exercise in the fashion that Bootsie did. Just the thought of spending three to four hours on the spinning wheel, even if she had that much time in her day, bored Harriet beyond belief.

"Well," she thought to herself, "here I am bruised, sweaty, embarrassed, stressed and feeling like a failure, and I still have most of my day ahead of me! And, now I've missed lunch as well!"

If there's one thing Harriet knew about herself, it was that she became really cranky if she didn't get to eat some lunch. With any luck, she'd be the only hamster in history to overdose on serotonin and endorphins just from the effort to get herself back to her office in one piece.

"Bootsie," Harriet said with conviction, "it's time this hamster got off the wheel."

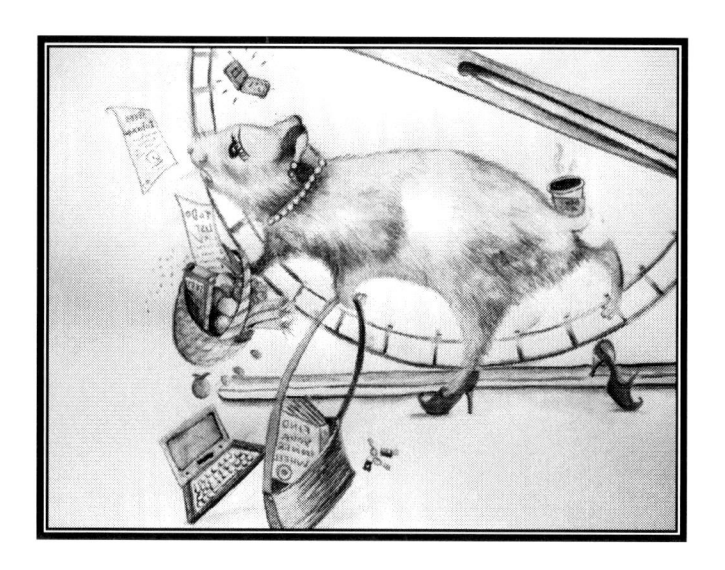

Take the Wheel

Enjoy Your Physical Power!

What are your feelings about your physical body? Your wonderful body is a profoundly complex mechanism that has supported you through all the adventures of your life. When you enjoy your *Physical Power* you move with greater confidence and presence. It isn't about exercise but about being comfortable in the body you have and honoring its needs. Ask your body what it needs each day – you may be surprised at the answer!

Chapter 6

'TO DO or not TO DO, that is the question'

Something about her experience with Bootsie had instilled a kind of resolve in Harriet to find a solution that would really work for her. As she talked to more and more hamsters in the office, she realized she wasn't alone in feeling overburdened and exhausted from trying to do it all. During one such conversation Harriet was impressed by the comprehensive To Do lists that a few of her colleagues kept. Their To Do lists were prominently posted near their desks, with items checked off and updated on a daily basis.

"Do To Do lists really work?" Harriet asked Mason and Jerry, two particularly organized co-workers.

"Of course they work!" Mason, gray whiskers fluttering, said with an air of complete confidence. "These lists provide perfect order to our days. At any time I know what I have to do, what I've done and what I need from others to do what I have to do."

"They saved my life," offered Jerry. "Before I made my To Do lists, I felt completely out of control and unable to keep up with all the work I was being asked to complete. Why now I make my To Do list and download it to my h-pad so I have my list with me wherever I go. I upload it again at the end of the day, print it out and put it up near my desk to get that sense of satisfaction as items get marked **DONE**."

Harriet thought about that. If it worked for Mason and Jerry, then perhaps it would work for her. She decided to learn the basics of good To Do list maintenance and then set off to put into practice what she had learned.

Harriet had to admit that her first To Do list was a very satisfying experience. It took her about an hour to get her list set up and organized but, when she was done, she really felt better. Just seeing everything she needed to worry about all in one place, right in front of her, was somehow reassuring. It was as if the To Do list itself had some mysterious power to ensure that every item noted there would be done.

"It should be called the I'm Done list," Harriet thought, because she felt like she had actually taken a major step toward completing all the items she saw before her.

Just as she was admiring her list yet again, Harriet was interrupted by a call from her European counterpart on the company slogan market research project.

"Good Day, Harriet," Bruno began, "I must unfortunately report that we have to do away with the company slogan. It is simply an unworkable premise for the European community."

"What?" Harriet said. "What do you mean 'an unworkable premise?' What is the problem?"

"It's not just one problem, Harriet," her counterpart said, "it is the very essence of seeds themselves and what they mean to hamsters around the world. It just doesn't speak to us the way it does to you American hamsters. We would like to suggest a new slogan to be presented to management – one that would be highly marketable and prestigious anywhere in the world."

"And what would that be?" Harriet asked, trying to suppress just the slightest tinge of sarcasm.

"We think the slogan should be 'We have the seeds you need.' Wonderful, no?"

"Wonderful, no!" Harriet replied. "It doesn't mean the same thing at all. In fact, it is almost the same slogan as the original one – just a slight difference in wording."

"But, that's the point, Harriet," her colleague said. "We like the original slogan. It had dignity and clarity. The current slogan, 'Sow Your Seeds With Us,' . . . well, it conjures up images of rapacious hamsters copulating all over the company! It's undignified and completely unacceptable! What sort of message are we sending to the young hamsters of the world?"

Harriet couldn't believe her tingling pink ears. She tried to think of some logical argument to get the European team back on board with the project but to no avail. Every reasonable suggestion she made was met with derision, finally culminating in Bruno shouting into the phone:

"Why don't we just put a big picture in the annual report of naked hamsters spilling their seed all over the precious company wheel of progress!"

With that Harriet, having gnawed three pencils, one ruler and a table leg to shavings, gave up the fight.

Later that day, Harriet found herself in the precarious position of having to convey to the executive hamsters of the company that the Europeans felt their new slogan was a signal to the world that hamsters were completely out of control at Seeds International. Needless to say, this information was not well received, leading to a decision to have a massive training program for all employees to enlighten them not only as to the meaning of the new slogan but also as to how they should present it to key customers and business partners. This decision meant a lot more work for Harriet and her team; work the executive hamsters fully expected she would do while keeping to her market research deadlines.

By the time Harriet got finished with the European brouhaha, it was time to go home. The next day when she came in, Harriet realized that her To Do list would need to be expanded. After a few days, she noticed that she could practically paper the walls of her office with To Do lists and still not check off enough items to feel she was making progress. She then started splitting the lists into To Do and Not To Do lists, eventually finding some small measure of satisfaction in checking off the items on the Not To Do list as completed.

Ah . . . accomplishment at last.

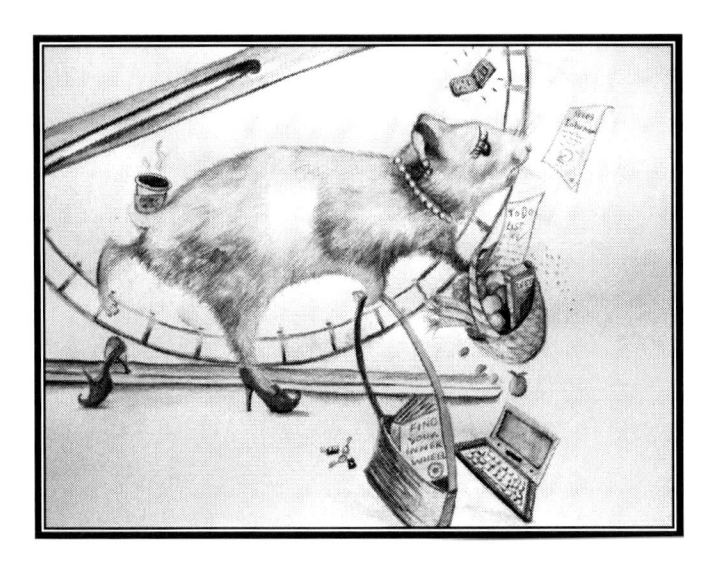

Take the Wheel

The Power of Delegation

What's on your To-Do List? By learning the *Power of Delegation* you can take back control of time and your day. Review what you have agreed to do and think about who could do that task for you. Whether it's time to finally get that cleaning crew for the house or ask a co-worker to attend a meeting that you don't really need to attend, chances are you take on way too much. Use the *Power of Delegation* to stay focused on your high-value activities. Do what only *you* can do.

Chapter 7

Harriet hadn't given up. When she was home over the weekend, she read in the Burrow News about a local hamster who had started a group program for stressed out corporate employees. Harriet decided to give it a try. It was at the **Om Hoga** center near her office where she had once taken a pawlates class, and there was a meeting Harriet found she could attend on her lunch hour. That first day Harriet arrived a little early, wanting to get a good seat and an early look at her fellow hamsters. While she waited Harriet looked at the posters for the *hoga* (Hamster yoga) classes offered during the afternoon and evening hours. There were hamsters in every position imaginable; in positions Harriet didn't even realize hamsters could get into. Most of all, hoga enthusiasts eschewed the wheel – seeing it as an archaic symbol of physiology over free will. Hoga devotees aspired to be one with the great wheel of creation, preferring the symbolic essence of the cyclical nature of all life to the tangible reality of metal and steel that most hamsters had in their homes. Harriet thought about how omnipresent the wheel seemed to be in all hamsters' lives.

Her reverie was interrupted by a large shout of:

"The wheel is not destiny!"

This was said by a young hamster who had come up to the front of the seated group. Harriet assumed he must be the leader of the program. He was dressed rather strangely, wearing a skirt-like lower garment, a tee shirt and an expensive looking silk tie around his head like a bandana. His fur was a beautiful golden brown and his black eyes showed the intensity of a hamster on a mission. Most of the attendees applauded his appearance but Harriet decided to reserve judgment. She was still trying to figure out his outfit.

"Freedom! Freedom my fellow hamsters!" he was saying, "Tear off the uniform of enslavement. The wheel is not destiny!"

A roar went up from the group. Harriet felt a little uncomfortable. But she had come to learn what she could, so she decided to try to understand what he was saying. At least now she knew the reason for his unusual garb. He was making a statement of sorts – Harriet just wasn't sure that his new choice of wardrobe was making a better statement – or any statement at all other than telling the world he couldn't dress himself.

"There you go again, Harriet," she caught herself, "try not to be so cynical."

"Let's begin," the leader was saying, "please each introduce yourself – first names only remember – and tell us why you are here."

With that one hamster after another stood up, said their name, and proclaimed:

"I am addicted to the wheel."

When it was Harriet's turn, she stood and introduced herself and said:

"I'm not sure if I'm addicted to the wheel or not. I'm not really sure what this program is about, but I do know I'm tired and exhausted all the time and need help getting back control of my life."

At the mention of the word, 'control,' a murmur went up from the group. The leader held up his paws to shush the members.

"Welcome, Harriet," he said, "we applaud your courage in coming today. If you will but follow the program, you will get the answers you seek."

By the end of the introduction, Harriet had sorted out the approach of the program. Success was to be achieved by admitting one had no control over the wheel and accepting that only the *Great Wheel* held the answers. This was coupled with various hoga postures done while breathing in the energy of the *Great Wheel* in order to feel energized, centered and stress-free. Most of all they were advised to stay away from any hamster-made wheels as undermining their oneness with the wheel of all creation. If they did this, the leader promised, their inner wheel would become strong, keeping them balanced throughout the day.

"Do I have an inner wheel?" Harriet thought to herself.

The next day, Harriet began her practice of hoga in earnest.

"The wheel is not destiny. The wheel is not destiny," she repeated over and over to herself while trying as best she could to stand on one leg and hold the other behind her back somewhere up around her shoulder blades. Hoga was much more difficult than Harriet had imagined but she stuck with it, contorting herself into all sorts of shapes. She was pretty sore most of the time but was assured that this would stop in a couple of weeks.

Harriet's real problem was she seemed unable to complete the class and stay awake at the same time. The last part of the hoga exercise was a relaxation done while lying on the floor. The first day, Harriet made it through the entire relaxation and had just started drifting off to sleep when the class was over. The second day she fell asleep somewhere towards the end of the guided session, while listening to the steady, monotonous tones of the instructor's voice. By the fifth day, Harriet fell asleep the minute her head hit the floor and other members began to complain that her loud snoring was disrupting their moments of serenity and oneness. By the end of week two, Harriet was skipping much of the actual exercise, choosing instead to go right to the floor position and let the music and soft tones of the instructor lull her to sleep. At the end of week three, the instructor, with urging from the entire class, asked Harriet to leave.

"It would seem that all I really got out of this program," Harriet thought to herself, "was a good nap in the middle of the day." Harriet's inner wheel, it seemed, just needed a bit of a rest.

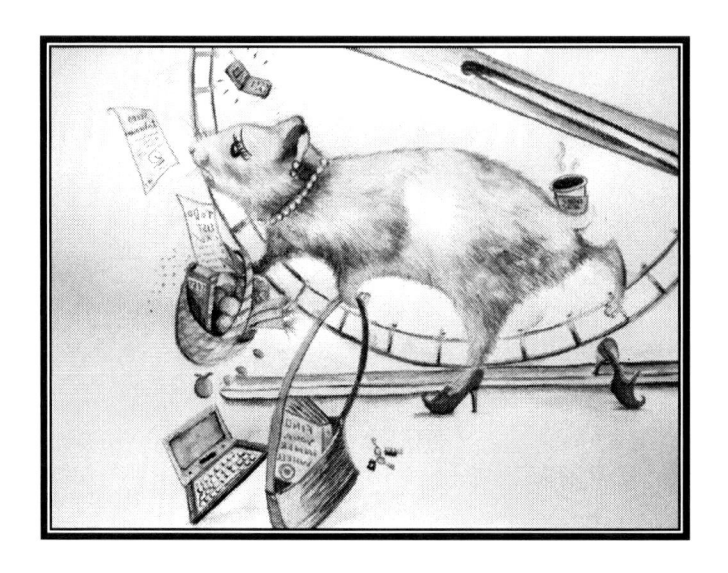

Take the Wheel

Use the Power of a Time-Out

Are you sleep-deprived and running on empty most of the time? If so, then you need to reconnect with the *Power of a Time-Out* to restore and replenish. Whether you meditate, do yoga or just like to walk the dog – the activity isn't as important as the time with your own being to quiet the mind and be present in the experience of the moment. Make the *Power of a Time-Out* part of your daily routine.

Chapter 8

After a particularly busy and tension-filled day at the office, Harriet came home to a den in chaos. Mitzi, her grape-stained brow hair illuminated by the waning sun streaming in the burrow doorways, was yelling that no one understood her. Bud was locked in his room playing the latest BattleHam video, and Walter was galloping after Mitzi matching her yell for yell. As Harriet crossed the threshold of the supposed sanctuary of her personal life, something in her snapped. She put her briefcase down in the entry way, turned around, shut the door and walked to the park by the river where she sat on a bench, alternating between thoughts of throwing herself in or throwing in everyone else she knew.

While she sat feeling somewhat comforted by the steady rhythm of the river, she noticed a hamster sitting out on the dock that jutted into the river. Now that wasn't unusual, but it was the expression on the face of this particular hamster that got Harriet's attention. There was a middle-aged hamster, dressed much like herself, sitting comfortably on the dock looking at the river with the most peaceful expression on her face.

"Hmmmph," Harriet thought, "she must not be a working hamster. Most likely, she is one of those society bluebloods who belongs to all the hamster philanthropic organizations and has only the stress of deciding how much money to give away to which charity."

For a brief moment, Harriet considered whether there was any possibility she could make herself into a believable charity. She blushed a bit, feeling guilty about her thoughts, when the hamster she had been watching got up and made her way back down the path from the dock, passing right by the bench Harriet was sitting on.

"You're just missing the magic word, my dear," she said as she paused just in front of Harriet.

For a moment Harriet didn't even realize she had been spoken to. Then she reacted as if someone had thrown cold water in her face.

"Do I know you?" she asked the serene hamster in front of her.

"You don't know me, my dear, but I know you. And countless more like you."

Harriet looked long and hard at the hamster face in front of her. She supposed she should be feeling afraid, but she was more curious than anything.

"What did you mean about a secret word?" she asked the serene stranger.

"My dear one, if you really want to change things, then take tomorrow off and meet me here by the river at 8:00am. I'll let you know what I've learned, including the magic word."

Harriet was about to protest that she couldn't possibly take the day off with all the work waiting for her at the office but something made her catch herself.

"I'll be there," she said to the stranger in front of her, "8:00am sharp!"

* * * * *

For some reason, Harriet was as excited the next morning as she could remember being for quite a long while. She was at the river at 8:00am sharp as she had promised, waiting for the serene stranger she met the day before, to appear. At a few minutes after 8 o'clock, there she was, walking slowly towards Harriet, a smile playing about her lips. Harriet was struck, as she had been the other day, by the sable-coated hamster's elegance and grace. She noticed the flecks of white in the dark fur, giving away her companion's true age.

Introducing herself as Henrietta, she said: "Well, Harriet, are you ready for your adventure?"

Harriet assured her she was and they set off together. Harriet was surprised to find herself a short while later in one of the large playgrounds situated around the park and the river. While they walked, Harriet learned that the mysterious Henrietta was in town on business and just happened to come by the river to watch the sunset – something she told Harriet she likes not to miss each and every day. Harriet, in turn, shared the story of her life, including how overwhelmed she had been feeling at work and at home. Harriet was usually a pretty private hamster but something about Henrietta made Harriet want to open up. Finally Henrietta stopped at a picnic table just outside the border of the playground and motioned Harriet to sit and join her.

"So, Harriet," she said, "let me see if I understand your problem. You have a very responsible job for a large, global company – a job you are good at, that you enjoy for the most part and which pays you a nice salary; a salary you and your husband Walter need to manage your household. You have two teenage hamsters scheduled to the max, who are acting out more and more at home and at school. You work a tremendous amount of overtime and are expected to be accessible even on your time off, including weekends and vacations. And, for some strange reason, you find yourself unhappy, tired, depleted and irritable a good portion of the time."

Harriet didn't appreciate what she took to be Henrietta's sarcasm at the end of her summary. Listening to someone else summarize her life in a few sentences made Harriet feel very small and insignificant. Her story didn't sound so bad when Henrietta told it. Harriet felt like even more of a failure complaining about her life.

"I always feel like I'm letting everyone down, Henrietta," Harriet said, "I try so hard to be the very best at work, the very best mother and wife and yet, I can't seem to keep up. I feel like I belong in a circus, not as the juggling act but as one of the clowns – you know – the one who keeps trying to get something to work but keeps getting run over by the toy car."

Henrietta smiled and said:

"You have been letting someone down, Harriet – someone very important – and the longer you ignore her, the more depressed and unhappy you're going to be."

"Oh, no, Henrietta," Harriet said, "don't tell me I have to find my inner hamster. I've been there and my inner hamster is as stressed as my outer hamster."

Henrietta laughed a long, hearty laugh and made Harriet smile in the process.

"Harriet, it's really not so complicated," Henrietta said. "In an attempt to be all things to others, it is inevitable that we let ourselves down. You must first be responsible to yourself. You must be your own first priority. If you will but do that, all your other responsibilities and priorities will fall into place."

Henrietta explained that it was no accident that she chose the playground for her meeting with Harriet.

"Think back to the beginning, Harriet," Henrietta said. "We come into the world as a bundle of needs – needs which we fully expect those who care for us to meet. We learn, however, to push our needs aside in order to meet expectations of our families, teachers and society. By the time we are grown, and this is especially true for female hamsters, it's a wonder we know where we begin and another ends, so intertwined have our lives become."

"But, Henrietta," Harriet was saying, "are you suggesting that we should be selfish and only think about ourselves? Who will want to be around us if we are only thinking about ourselves all the time?"

Henrietta asked Harriet to tell her the most selfish thing she has ever done. After several minutes, Harriet had to admit that she couldn't think of anything truly significant. So Henrietta gave Harriet a list of questions to answer. Some of the questions were getting Harriet quite perturbed.

"This one, Henrietta," Harriet said, "is just impractical. Here you ask, 'If invited to a family function, like a wedding, graduation or pup shower, and you don't want to go, are you being selfish refusing?'!"

"Why does that one bother you so much, Harriet?" Henrietta asked.

"It bothers me because I see where you're going with this, but you are overlooking the fact that sometimes we have to do things we don't want to do because of family duty and obligation. Are we to just throw those values away?" Harriet was flushed and getting more flushed by the minute.

"Harriet," Henrietta began, "just consider for a moment what things would be like if duty began and ended with duty to the self? I don't mean this in the sense of unkindness or insensitivity to others. I mean it in the sense of understanding what we each really need to feel fulfilled and content in life. I think you have made an assumption that many hamsters make – that it is not possible to fulfill one's own life unless it comes at the expense of others. Yet, living fully takes nothing away from anyone else. In fact, it is a great gift we can give to those we love and care for. Tell me how you normally handle declining functions that you truly don't want to attend."

"Well, that's easy," Harriet said, "I usually don't decline because I don't want to hurt anyone's feelings. So I just sit and hope I'll come down with a convenient sniffle right around the time I'm supposed to go. Or maybe a simple little mishap – nothing too serious – perhaps I trip and my back goes out. Everyone understands back pain. Or better yet, perhaps one of the pups or Walter comes down with something so I can stay home and take care of them. That way I can honestly say I would love to be there but my family comes first! You give me any situation and I can stretch it into something that causes me to stay home!"

"My goodness, Harriet!" Henrietta laughed. "You are certainly creative. Look at all the energy you put into coming up with good excuses!"

"Well," Harriet replied, "if you must know, I'm considered something of a genius when it comes to getting out of things. Other hamsters consult me for good excuses when they have obligations they can't figure out how to avoid."

Henrietta and Harriet were both laughing now.

"Harriet," Henrietta began when she caught her breath again, "do you have any idea how much effort is involved in what you currently do? No wonder you feel exhausted."

"I know, I know!" Harriet said, tongue firmly in cheek. "If only I could use my awesome power for good!"

"Well, Harriet," Henrietta responded. "I suggest we start channeling that wonderful sense of humor into areas that will nourish and not deplete you. But that will take some changes in the way you have been doing things. I think, however, the results will be more than you hoped for."

Harriet was open to ideas of change. She was very skeptical, however. Her sense of duty and obligation was all tied up with worries over what others would think of her. Harriet realized that much of her life had been spent meeting the expectations not of herself but of others and that some part of her was afraid to do otherwise.

This realization led to a long discussion with Henrietta about the obligations of love and family – about what we truly owe to each other and what we truly owe to ourselves. After a while Harriet began to shift her thinking a little bit.

"I guess it is a little crazy," she admitted, "that I sit hoping something bad will happen to me just so I can feel good about staying home!"

"It's more than a little crazy, Harriet." Henrietta said. "What we're talking about represents the core of why you feel so out of control in your life. It's the key to the problems at work and the problems at home. So, it's time to roll up your sleeves. If you really want things to change, then let's get to work!"

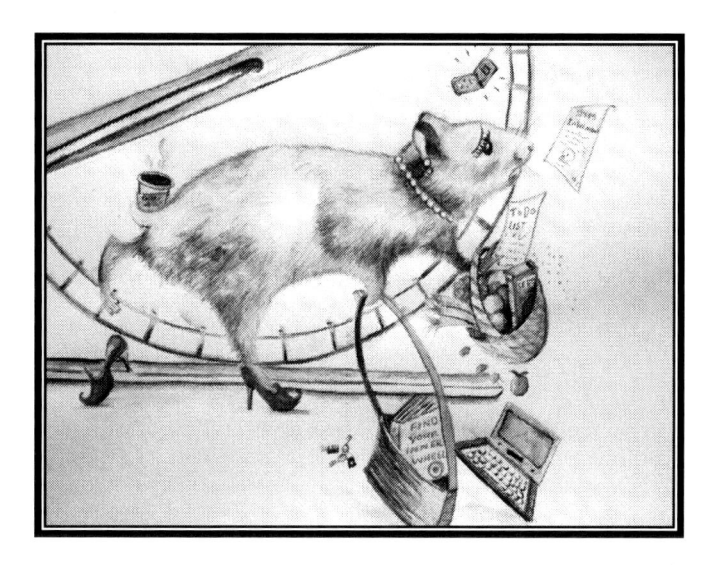

Take the Wheel

The Power of Self-Love

As a woman you may find it difficult to act in your own best self-interest. But your life is in no one else's hands. Every time you deny your own needs because you "have to" please someone else, you create the very stress you are trying to escape. From now on replace the words "I have to" with the words "I choose to". It will keep you aware in the present of your own true needs in any situation. Use the power of self-love to give yourself permission to be fulfilled.

Chapter 9

Harriet spent the rest of the morning, with Henrietta's help, making a list of obligations, at work and at home, that she felt she couldn't refuse, yet which she didn't really want to do. On the list were such diverse activities as helping Mitzi with a last minute project for school, picking up and dropping off Walter's dry cleaning, attending meetings at work which didn't contribute to her responsibilities, or projects that slipped in with no particular priority that caused consistent overtime. After each one Henrietta instructed Harriet to think of someone who could refuse the obligation and what sense of self that hamster might have that would allow for a different perspective. As Harriet worked through each item on her list, she realized the qualities needed were the same in each case. In each case what would allow Harriet to refuse obligations she didn't really want to take on was a sense of giving herself permission to put herself first – ahead of whatever it was she was being asked to do.

Harriet also began to realize that the reason she was reluctant to refuse such obligations was the same – fear that she would be somehow ostracized for her position. Harriet realized she feared the loss of love from Walter and the family if she didn't continue to meet their needs, even when those needs overshadowed her own. She feared loss of her job or her standing in the company if she didn't take on everything asked of her at work. With Henrietta's help, Harriet started to become aware that she somehow got something out of feeling so overextended. She had unwittingly become comfortable with an image of herself as the one who is always there for others – and her sense of self was so tied up in that image that it made it very hard for Harriet to think about putting her own needs first. She was very invested in her image at work of being the 'go-to' hamster to make sure major projects got done. Harriet was beginning to realize that making the changes Henrietta was suggesting was going to require that she face down her fears; and she was beginning to wish she had never embarked on this path.

Just as Harriet was mulling over the effort that would need to be involved to really change her life, Henrietta reached over and took her paw in both of hers.

"Harriet," she said, "I know it's difficult. I know you are wondering if this is worth rocking the boat at work and at home. You're thinking that you have managed so far and that it might just be easier to keep going the way you have been. You're even telling yourself that no one is really happy and fulfilled in life. Who are you to expect that you can pull this off?"

Harriet nodded and felt tears come to her eyes.

"It will be difficult, Harriet," Henrietta was continuing, "in fact, it might just be the most difficult thing you have ever done. But at the end you will have emerged stronger, more content and surer of yourself than you will have ever believed possible. You may lose some friends along the way but many more will come to fill their places – many who will support and honor the new Harriet and accept her for whom she is, not for what she does for them."

The rest of the afternoon Harriet, with Henrietta's continued help and encouragement, worked on writing down her commitments to herself. Henrietta had Harriet create a chart with five headings. Each heading represented an area of life that Henrietta wanted Harriet to review. In essence the chart was a visual reminder for Harriet that her life was potentially so much richer and full than she might have realized. As Harriet looked at the chart, she considered each heading carefully.

Harriet took her list of obligations or activities that she would like to stop doing and organized each item under the appropriate heading. One thing Henrietta pointed out to Harriet right away was how the lists under work and family were extensive while there was very little under health, play and spirit. No wonder Harriet had been feeling so depleted and exhausted. She had neglected to make investments in the most important areas of her life – those that helped her connect with who she truly was.

Life Area	Fulfillment Qualities
Work	Meaningful Contribution
Friends & Family	Meaningful Relationships
Health	Physical, Mental, Emotional Well-Being
Play	Creative Self-Expression
Spirit	Self-Actualization

Henrietta explained that each of the five areas needs to be kept in focus every day in order to live with balance – not equality; balance. Henrietta was very clear that the goal was not to devote equal time to each area. In fact, time itself was not a consideration in Henrietta's scheme. Instead the consideration was around making self-motivated lifestyle changes that yielded a sense of empowerment and choice.

The hardest part for Harriet was realizing that she would have to let go of the guilt that came from not doing everything that everyone else needed. For so long Harriet had defined herself in terms of others. It was a new and radical idea to put herself first. But something about Henrietta's approach made sense to Harriet in a way that all the other methods she had tried didn't. Henrietta explained that all the other approaches were merely tools – tools that became effective once you knew what truly mattered to you and were willing to act on your own behalf. On their own, none held the answer, and sometimes even added to feelings of inadequacy.

Harriet and Henrietta worked well into the evening; Harriet's comfort growing with each passing hour. By the end of the day, Harriet felt clearer in mind and lighter in heart than she had in a very long while. She was still apprehensive but couldn't wait to put what she had learned about herself today into practice. She knew it wasn't going to easy – it wasn't an overnight fix – but she saw that if she just stayed the course, she would eventually accomplish what she now knew she wanted.

As Harriet walked Henrietta back to her hotel and thanked her with a hug, she remembered that Henrietta had never given her the magic word she promised. She asked Henrietta what the magic word was and Henrietta explained that until now, Harriet wouldn't have understood the power of the magic word and been unable to use it. With that, Henrietta whispered the magic word in Harriet's ear and said a final farewell.

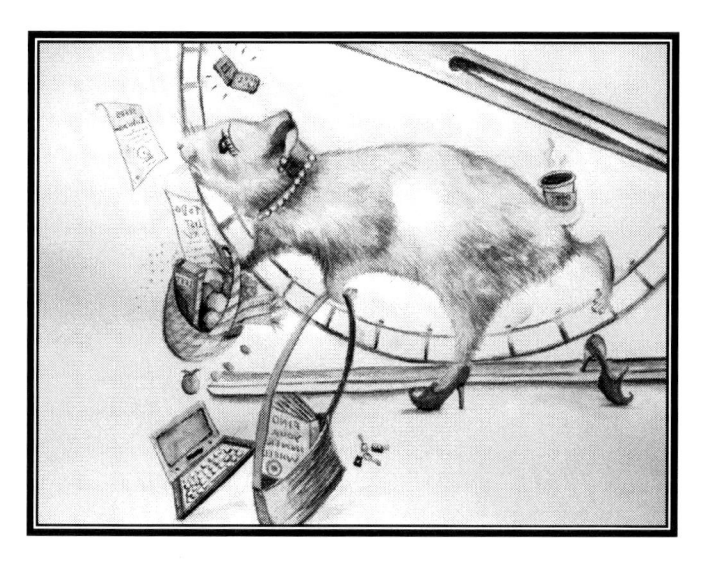

Take the Wheel

The Power of Choice

No power is more significant than the power of Choice. It is the single most empowering opportunity you have, and you have lots of those opportunities every day from the food you choose to eat to the workload you take on. Every time you use your "no" to decline something you don't want to do you open up your universe to what truly matters to you. You start to give to yourself in a very real way and find your "yes" becomes a selective treasure that brings you real pleasure and joy.

Chapter 10

A new day had dawned in Harriet Hamster's household and the effects were sending shockwaves through the other members of the family.

"What do you mean, you won't help me finish my project for science class?" asked an incredulous Mitzi.

"I'm sorry, Mitzi," Harriet explained, "but you let it go to the last minute and I am not going to stay up until the wee hours of the morning to compensate for that. I've decided I need my sleep. In the future, I would be happy to help you but you must do your own work first and not expect me to step in and rescue you."

Mitzi was crying, saying how unfair Harriet was being; how she didn't love Mitzi anymore. Harriet, proudly, withstood it all.

"The answer is still no, Mitzi," Harriet said, "no matter how much you carry on. I suggest you come clean with your teacher tomorrow morning, accept the mark you have earned and ask if you can do extra work to pull up your grade."

Harriet was still unsteady using the magic word. Like Henrietta had warned her, it held power beyond belief. As Mitzi stormed off to her room to face the consequences of her procrastination, Harriet felt a sense of calm come over her. It had been a few weeks since her talk with Henrietta and it was only now that Harriet could use the magic word without feeling guilty. She had started practicing her newfound methods on Walter one morning.

"Walter," Harriet said, "please pick up the dry cleaning on your way home from work today."

"What?" Walter said, looking up from reading the Burrow News on his h-pad. "Why do you want me to pick up the dry cleaning? You always do that."

"I used to do that, Walter, but since you pass the dry cleaners on your drive home, I think it makes sense that you pick it up and drop it off from now on." Harriet waited for Walter's reaction.

"Well, I can do it *today*," Walter carefully said, "if it would help you out, but I'm not so sure I want to do it all the time."

"Well, Walter," Harriet said, "I'm not sure I want to do it all the time either, but I always have. If you want to continue to have your suits and shirts dry cleaned, then this will be your responsibility from now on."

"Hold on there, Harriet," Walter was saying, the pitch of his voice rising a little, "as I said, I don't mind helping out but I have a busy work day and look forward to coming home to relax, not run errands."

"Walter," Harriet said, pulling herself up to her full height and fluffing her fur, "we share the responsibilities of taking care of what needs to be done around here. I know I haven't asked that much of you before and that has been my fault. We're partners, Walter. Let's start acting that way."

Walter looked at Harriet like he had never seen her before and, Harriet thought to herself, his expression wasn't exactly one of overwhelming appreciation and newfound respect.

Walter decided to test Harriet's resolve.

"Harriet, I certainly agree that we are partners and agree I need to do more. I am comfortable with that as long as you agree to pitch in when I get stuck at work or perhaps on those Saturdays that I have my mini-golf game planned." Walter thought this was eminently reasonable.

"No, Walter," Harriet said, trying out the magic word for the first time. "You will just have to plan around those times when work is busy, or when you have arranged to play mini-golf to make sure you get everything done. If not, it will just wait until the next week." Harriet let out a deep breath.

Walter was getting upset. He had expected Harriet to cave in and agree to pitch in if he were busy. Walter knew, but wasn't sure Harriet knew, that he had tried to start her down a slippery slope of taking things over again. She had held firm. As he looked at Harriet, Walter felt his anger starting to rise. Why should he have to change? Haven't things been working just fine? He knew Harriet had been feeling tired but she always managed to get everything done. Walter wasn't at all sure he liked this new Harriet!

Unbeknownst to Walter, after their exchange Harriet had walked out, gone down to sit by the river, and repeated the magic word over and over again in her mind until the guilt she was feeling about asking Walter to do more had passed.

"No! No! No! No!" Harriet said to herself over and over. She then went over the commitments that she had made to herself in her mind. To those she affirmed, "Yes! Yes! Yes! Yes!" Henrietta had taught Harriet that she must first say, 'yes,' to herself and her priorities before she could say 'no,' to others.

Over the next few months, Harriet felt like she was in a battle zone at home. Walter blew up the first time he forgot to pick up his suits and shirts at the dry cleaners and blamed Harriet for the problem. With Walter this was just the tip of the iceberg, and he and Harriet had many more animated discussions about responsibilities around the house. Mitzi and Bud continued to test Harriet's resolve by not doing their homework, forgetting books they needed for tests, and even by staying out and not calling on a school night. When Harriet would once again refuse to write a report for her for school, Mitzi would text Harriet at work conveying her outrage. An onslaught of buzzing would have Harriet looking down only to see 4COL (*for crying out loud!*) or YGTBKM (*you've got to be kidding me!*). Harriet simply texted back OYO (*on your own*) until Mitzi finally surrendered.

As she made the changes in her life that she realized were necessary, Harriet had to steel herself to withstand what felt like the withdrawal of the love she had come to count on. Without even knowing they were doing it, Walter and the pups played every guilt card in the deck and Harriet spent many an hour secretly crying her eyes out. But slowly, ever so slowly, things started to settle down. When they did, Harriet realized that everyone ultimately benefited. By just changing herself, Harriet had started a domino effect of change in everyone in the family – changes that ultimately were for the better but which were extremely difficult in the process.

There came a day when Mitzi truly started to take responsibility for her school work and drew up some real goals about what she wanted for college. Bud, finally out of clothes after Harriet stopped doing his laundry, grudgingly gave in and actually learned how to use the washing machine and dryer. With Walter, responsibilities weren't shared equally but that wasn't the important thing. Now both Harriet and Walter had an appreciation of what was done and had worked through a process of negotiation and acceptance. Harriet still did more around the house than Walter but both felt acknowledged and appreciated for what they did. Harriet was more than satisfied with the changes being made at home. Little did she know that it would be work that would pose the greatest challenge!

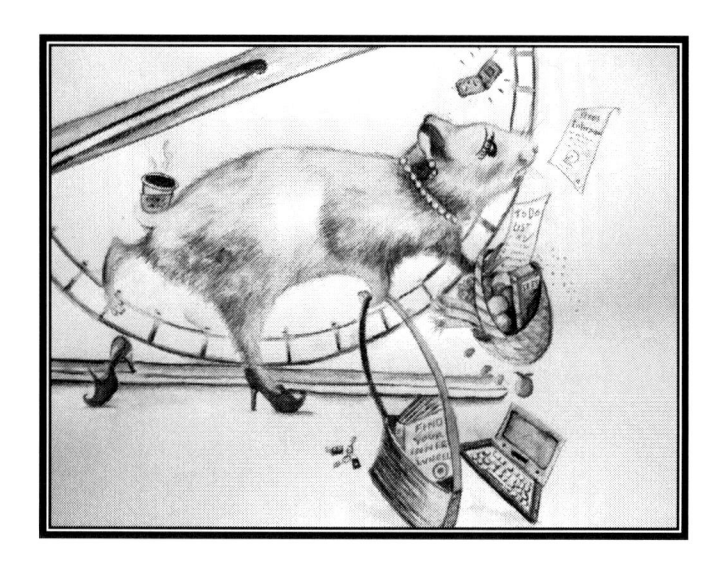

Take the Wheel

The Power of Balance

Once the Power of Choice is mastered, balance becomes something you create on a daily basis. Some days you may choose to give your energy to a new project at work; some days to a special evening with your spouse or partner; some days to a massage after work; some days to a board game with the kids. As you create balance you will become better able to help your children and loved ones also use the power of self-love and choice. Imagine how amazing that gift would be!

Chapter 11

At work Harriet felt she still had a ways to go. The changes she was making weren't exactly being warmly embraced. And, to her own surprise, she found it much harder to say her magic word at work than she had at home. As a first step in her plan, Harriet had stopped going to meetings that she felt she needn't attend and delegated appropriate responsibility to her staff. She decided that each person who worked for her needed to be fully responsible for themselves and their work so she stopped double-checking what was being done and allowed them to learn from their mistakes. This was probably the hardest change Harriet made. She had feared mistakes for so long that it tied her stomach up in knots the first time something went wrong. Harriet also stopped checking her work-related emails, texts and voice mails on the weekends and evenings. She let her staff and management know about this change, and when pressured, calmly said:

"No. That is my time with my family. Whatever it is can wait until the following day or the Monday after the weekend."

Willy and Sten pulled her aside after a staff meeting.

"Harriet," Sten said, "you're killing your career here. Everyone is expected to work as much overtime as needed and be accessible on a 24-hour basis. Management is starting to say you have no 'urgency' about your work. You know what that means!"

"That may be what has been expected," Harriet replied, "but I need time for myself, my family and my interests. I've decided to meet my expectations first and let others adjust theirs as need be."

Willy and Sten weren't wrong. Harriet took a lot of heat over her new attitude and even sat by and watched another get the promotion she had been promised just a year before. The day came when Percy, her Hamsters Resource Representative, called her into his office.

"Harriet, Harriet, Harriet . . ." Percy was shaking his head. "I've been hearing some disturbing things about you lately."

Harriet thought that if Percy looked any more serious, she would have to pinch herself to make sure she hadn't passed on.

"For goodness sake, Percy!" Harriet said. "You look like you're about to give my eulogy."

"There it is again, Harriet," Percy said, "I don't understand this sense of humor of yours. This is serious business. I'm told you are refusing to be available away from the office and have stopped double and triple-checking the work of those who report to you. Why, just the other day, Sten, your direct report, made a mistake on his market share update!" Percy said this last sentence as if this was the first time any mistake had ever happened in the entire history of the company.

Harriet's mind was spinning out all sort of clever retorts. Well, let's just hold a public flogging in the cafeteria she wanted to say, but stopped herself just in time. Instead she actually managed to keep a straight face when she answered Percy.

"I know these changes aren't easy, Percy. They're not easy for me as well. But my very sanity is at stake and I truly believe my work is not only better because of the changes I am making but that I am more consistently productive than I've been in a very long time."

Harriet might as well have been talking to the potted plant on the window sill behind Percy. As she sat there Harriet was told she was not meeting expectations, even though those expectations could not be expressed in any specific way. She was even told that perhaps Seeds International wasn't the right company for her – a thinly veiled threat that had her in fear of losing her job. That was one of the hardest moments for Harriet in her change process. She questioned whether she was truly doing the right thing. But she had come so far that she just couldn't go back now to the way she had been. Whatever happened, Harriet had begun the process of reclaiming her life and enough benefit was being felt to keep her motivated and persevering through the setbacks.

Again, just like in her family, little by little, everyone around Harriet managed to adjust. A year or two went by and then – a funny thing happened. The company executives noticed Harriet in a way they had not noticed her before. Harriet was becoming known as the hamster who managed to do quality work (her staff too!) without a lot of overtime and high anxiety and stress. The executives started talking to each other about how Harriet must be a natural leader. After all, she knew when to make the tough decisions – when to say no. They respected that in a hamster.

Over the next few years, Harriet was given increasingly responsible positions in the company. Each time, Harriet checked in with herself to see if she wanted the advancement. Knowing she could always set her limits gave Harriet the freedom to try new things. She no longer feared she would fail. She knew the secret. If she just stuck to putting herself and her needs first then she would clearly know how to fit everything else in. Not every day was perfect, but most days were more than just okay. Most days Harriet was very content with her life and the choices she made.

Finally Harriet was asked to replace the retiring CEO of Seeds International. As she met with the Board of Hamsters, Harriet told them she would accept the position with a few changes. For one thing, Harriet did not want the lucrative executive salary and options normally given to the CEO. She proposed a much more modest compensation package, one that had the board members shaking their heads.

"Harriet," the senior board member said, "hamsters are hoarders. It's what we do. The only reason most of us want to continue to move up in a company is so we will finally have all that we need. Hoarding is a natural instinct. You can't seriously propose that someone can be a CEO and not be a hoarder at the same time."

A murmur went up around the room. The subject was clearly making the board members uncomfortable.

"Yes, we are hoarders," Harriet answered, "but we used to hoard just to make sure we got through a difficult winter when food was scarce. Now we hoard just to hoard, and when we do that, we never have enough. I don't need everything you have offered. In fact, I don't want everything you have offered. I want to be able to share the profits of Seeds International with the hamsters who have helped make them; and if that means that less comes to me so more can go to them, then so be it. I tell you what. Let me have the job for a year. If you don't see a more profitable company after one year, then I will gladly step down."

The board members asked Harriet to leave while they discussed her proposal. Even though they couldn't condone her approach, they decided to give her the year she requested. She would learn they believed that even **she** was a hoarder at heart.

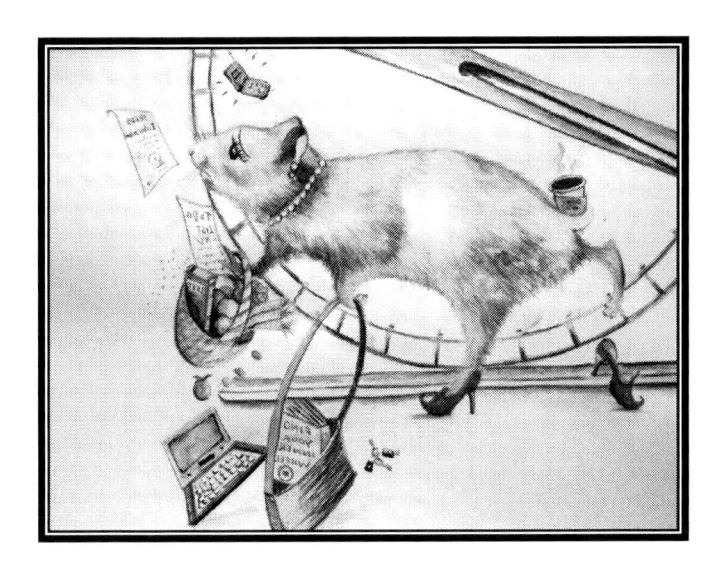

Take the Wheel

The Power of Perseverance

Change isn't easy and not always embraced by friends, family and colleagues. As you change you create ripple effects – some will be welcomed; others not. Once you know your deepest needs and what you need to live a fulfilled life it's time to use the power of perseverance to move forward daily towards your goals. Perseverance demonstrates your commitment through the ups and downs of change to your own vision for your life. Be kind to yourself and just keep moving ahead – one small action at a time.

Chapter 12

Harriet had been CEO of Seeds International for five years now, and in those five years, the company had prospered and her hamsters had prospered in ways they had not even thought possible. One of the first things Harriet had done with the money not given to her for executive compensation was to raise the topic of work/life balance to the level of a core business strategy. She was the prime executive sponsor of the initiative along with the various business heads and spent considerable time crafting the strategy and associated competencies, performance measurements and review mechanisms to ensure it had the investment and senior management focus it would need to make a real change in the way the company approached the subject.

Out of the strategy came the creation of many services for hamsters to help them better manage their busy lives. One of the first was a group called **Hamster Helpers**, formed for a rather small investment. The purpose of this group, which consisted of retired hamsters, hamsters in college and stay-at-home parent hamsters, was to step in for a Seeds International employee at home when need be. So, a hamster helper would wait at your house for the washing machine technician so you didn't have to take a day off. Or perhaps stay home with your pups on a school holiday if you had a pressing business project you wanted to finish. The real benefit was that it was up to each hamster to choose when they needed a hamster helper so each could make the choices that best suited them.

There were many other changes as well: greater flexibility at all levels for working from home and job sharing; casual dress was the order of the day every day; every three years every hamster was required to take a six-week sabbatical in order to make sure she had time to reflect on her life and make the appropriate adjustments. Out of those sabbaticals came some of the great innovative ideas that continued to make the company grow and prosper. Standard training programs on time and stress management were replaced with life management courses that embodied the ideas and secrets that Henrietta had taught to Harriet so long ago. Harriet hadn't gone back to the outmoded idea of the company as family but she had realized that, for any company to keep the best hamsters in today's world, it had better make family a priority and provide the services and benefits that supported the multi-dimensional lives that most hamsters now lived.

Harriet also instituted new values for the company and made sure that the new values were lived at every level. She did this not with massive training programs but by example. As Harriet and the business leaders started living the life balance options they instituted and encouraged their organizations to do the same, hamsters lost their fear of setting priorities for themselves and began to naturally work together to find the best way to accomplish what they had to do, respecting their own and others' needs for time away from the office. By year three, Seeds International had been named as one of the best companies to work for by a majority of work/life balance consulting firms. This award was earned, while at the same time, the company was exceeding all measures of productivity and growth.

The large hamster wheel of progress was gone – a symbol, Harriet felt, that no longer represented the company's purpose. Instead Seeds International hamsters had a few short sentences on the back of their ID cards to remind them what the company stood for. If you stopped any one hamster and asked what it was that made Seeds International such a great company you would be told that every hamster has the right to say "no"; that no one hamster is more or less important than another; that mistakes were considered part of learning and innovation; and that each hamster was wholly responsible for his work. You would learn that empowerment was not just a word but a program lived on a daily basis.

Each hamster was encouraged to create the best life for herself and bring the highest and best of who she was to her work.

The competitors of Seeds International had watched with interest as Harriet became CEO. They watched as she instituted some unusual changes and waited for her to fail. Instead they found themselves losing more and more of their best people to Seeds International, as well as losing market share. They had laughed when Harriet replaced the company slogan, *Sow Your Seeds with Us* with a new one, *We Nourish the World*. But no one was laughing now, except perhaps Harriet. Harriet laughed a lot these days.

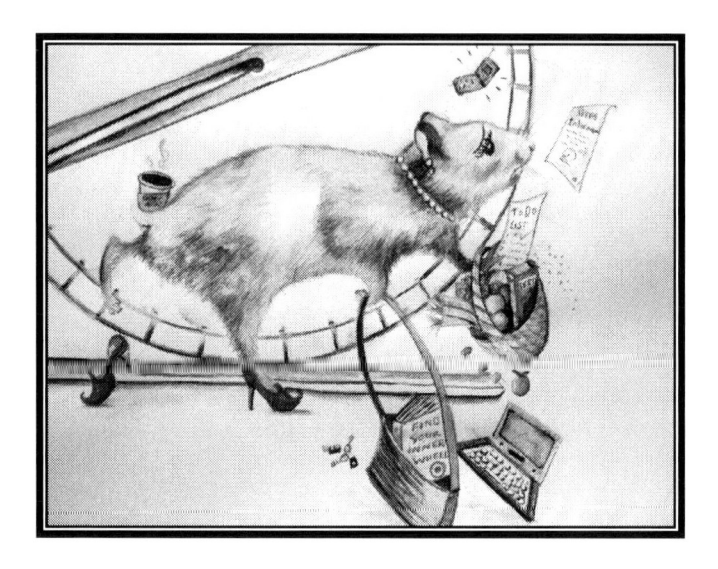

Take the Wheel

The Power of Creative Vision

Within you, whether you realize it or not, lies a vision for your life. And it is uniquely yours. No matter what your work you can use the power of your creative vision to better your environment. As you practice your powers of delegation, self-love, choice, balance, intention setting and perseverance you set in motion an energy that empowers not only yourself but everyone around you.

Chapter 13

After Laura finished reading, the group was silent for a bit. Rosemary finally broke the ice.

"I loved the part of the story about exercise and the time management courses. You know, now that I think about it, Harriet is right. Companies and well-meaning gurus focus on time management and stress management coping mechanisms as if that were the essence of the problem. I roared with laughter when Harriet fell off the wheel at the gym! I know exactly how she feels. Exercise has become one more thing I feel I 'should' do that adds to my feeling overwhelmed!"

The group began an animated discussion about Harriet's approach. Jane pointed out that the changes Harriet goes through turn out well – after all this is a fable and fables are about lessons and outcomes – though perhaps not always about reality. In reality, many who have tried to find a way to balance the demands of work and home life, don't achieve their goals. Many, in fact, end up leaving companies just as they are hitting their peak. This is especially true of women, who seem less and less willing to sacrifice a well-rounded personal life for success in the office.

Ronnie noted that even the terminology poses a problem. The very fact that we talk about work/life as two separate subjects is part of the problem. It confirms a duality that many accept but which is illusionary in nature.

Laura mentioned Henrietta's view that we each have only *one* life. And with that one life, we must balance our needs and the demands on our time across the dimensions of work, meaningful relationships, creative play, health and our spirit – the part of us that actualizes the very best we have to offer, that energizes us and gives us our vitality. It is the shift from living a life compartmentalized in buckets labeled 'work' and 'home' to a life lived within the flow of a day, a week, a month, a year. In each of those days, balance becomes the acknowledgement and allowing of our needs and priorities measured against the demands on our time and energy.

"The issue is not that work and life are on opposite ends of the scale, but that the 'self' is left out of the equation," Ronnie noted. "Like many women, my life is multi-dimensional and, at different times, each of these dimensions or components demands more time and attention than another. Any approach to work/life balance needs to have as its foundation, care of the self. We can't give to others, our careers and our health from an empty vessel. The trick is to nurture the self first and from that place of fullness, be able to give to all the other areas of our lives."

She looked over at the other women in the group.

"Let's face it. Putting themselves first is something men have always done very easily. It's time women made themselves their first priority."

"What?" Rosemary queried. "Put myself first? Not the children? Not my husband? Not the job? It gives me anxiety just to think about it!

"I understand completely, Ro." Laura replied. "As women we are so used to putting the needs of others before our own, that taking time to focus on ourselves as the priority seems selfish at best and negligent at worst. And it can feel damn uncomfortable to boot! Think about it. Women in our culture are the care takers – the ones whose job it is to keep everyone else in balance; however, the problem with that is, if you are the person keeping everyone else's life and emotions in balance, you are the one who is going to feel tired and sick."

Jane spoke up again.

"I think the most important lesson in Harriet's story is that there is no simple answer. You can't take a course to fix your life. And life balance isn't an equation. The goal isn't to devote equal time to each area. That means the answer is, of necessity, specific to the individual. The only solution that will really work is one that is customized by and for the individual. This is the first time that I've seen anyone propose a blueprint to help you do just that."

While the group pondered Jane's words, Laura started passing out large pieces of paper. Once everyone had a worksheet, Laura made her proposal.

"Let's see if what Jane says is right. Each make a chart with space for the five areas mentioned in the story – work, family, play (creativity), health and spirit. Under each heading list three obligations you currently have that you *have no real enthusiasm or energy* for. These are not survival things – like needing to nurse the baby but rather the things you do out of a sense of duty or obligation that don't feed your heart. Next, go through each one and jot down some ideas on how you can start saying 'no' to what you no longer want to do. Let's take it a step further, like Harriet did, and keep at it until we each figure out the payback we get from draining our energy in fulfillment of the expectations of others."

Quiet ensued as each person worked on her chart.

"You know," Jane interrupted, "writing down what I don't really enjoy doing is easy. I'm so familiar with what I don't like about my job and my life that just keeping the list down to three items each isn't easy!"

"Well, Jane, I find that the hard part comes next," Laura replied. "Once you have finished your lists, take a new worksheet, again with the same five headings across the top. But on this worksheet make a list under each heading of the things that give you joy – at work, with your family, in creative expression, with your health and your spirit. Once you've done that, identify at least one commitment you can make to yourself for change in each area to move more towards the things that give you joy rather than the things, activities and people who drain you."

A collective groan went up from the group.

"Here's where we run into the problem of what we can and cannot control about our situation." Rosemary spoke what everyone was thinking.

"Good point, Rosemary," Laura said, "so let's make sure the commitments are clearly within our span of control so we can have a reasonable level of confidence in our success."

Later that evening the group agreed that this was one of the best book club meetings they had had in quite some time.

"You know," Jane began, "that story got me thinking not only about what I can change for myself but also how I can influence the company to build some strategic thinking about the issue."

"I agree," Lily said, "as a CEO of a mid-size company myself, I have to admit I never really looked at work/life balance as something that needs to be elevated to the level of core business strategy. I cringed at the 'CEOs are hoarders' line. Yet even I feel that executive level compensation is out of control. I always felt work/life balance was an HR problem, best left to the specialists in that area. Harriet's story has gotten me thinking that, like any potentially successful business strategy, work/life balance needs sponsorship at the highest levels and performance measures that support the changes we are trying to make. If we don't raise it up and see it as a key investment area that pays dividends, we won't be ready to compete for the brightest entering the workforce and the very best that management has to offer."

"Lily, you implement something like what Harriet described and I'll come work for you in a minute!"

Everyone laughed at Ronnie's outburst.

"Well," Laura concluded, "it seems tonight's book club has given us all a lot to think about not only for ourselves but for the people in our organizations and companies. Even for me here at home, I've learned a lot tonight about why I've made the choices I have and what my goals really are. I suggest we table our regular book club and use this time each month to work with each other on our commitments and changes we want to make. If we support each other, then we are sure to succeed. I can't think of a better use of our time, can you?"

The group enthusiastically agreed. The evening broke up to the sound of peals of laughter as a bunch of ring tones and buzzing sounded all at once – a reminder of the ever-present expectation of always being reachable and responsive. To everyone's surprise, Rosemary simply turned off her phone and proudly announced:

"My first NO! Of course, it's going to drive me crazy wondering who was trying to reach me and why!

"Good for you, Ro," Laura laughed, "one small victory is better than none! Maybe next month you won't arrive looking like someone hooked up to life support!"

Smiling, Ro touched the hearts of all as she said:

"Yes. From now on, my life support will be right here."

Postscript

The methods described in Harriet's story are fairly simple but that doesn't mean they are easy. Only you know what it is that brings you joy – what feeds your spirit and motivates you. By rethinking the issue to be one of life priorities and healthy limits, time no longer becomes the enemy. Life shifts from areas compartmentalized into little boxes labeled work, kids, exercise, husband, wife, friends, relaxation, chores . . . . into a life with overlapping demands and needs that only you can sort out successfully. The most important relationship to get right is the one to the self. Out of that flows all other relationships. Using the magic word, as Harriet did, is not about restricting life but about opening it up – opening it up to what really matters, and doing so with purpose, intent and clarity.

So, remember, having it all is not the same as doing it all. It is the option and opportunity to decide where to devote your energy – what to pick up and what to let go. And no one else can make that decision for you.

Perhaps, just perhaps, you too can be a 'Harriet" and take control of the wheel of your life. And . . . in the process . . . create a life of personal and professional satisfaction. Not perfection, mind you – but deep, heartfelt, satisfaction.

With love,
Cathleen